THE OFFICIAL CAFAE LATTE COOKBOOK

By C.M. Alongi
and
MaryJanice Davidson

Table of Contents

Dedication(s)

To the D&D group, who have been gaming in our dining room for well over a decade. (The pic below is the scene of *so many* crimes.) I love how you guys are adults now and could be anywhere in the world, but still choose to come for D&D, Magic the Gathering, etc. I'm pretty sure the food was at least part of the draw, making all of you the perfect subjects on which to test these recipes. My love, always. – MaryJanice

To all my lovely guinea pigs—I mean, friends. Friends who taste-tested everything in this book. I'm sure it was a great sacrifice. – Christina

Introduction

Why are we writing this? Boredom? A cynical cash grab? We lost a bet?

All incorrect, but nice try. Anyone who has written a cookbook knows it's a boatload of work, hardly worth it if you're just in it for the money. Though I recommend it as a cure for boredom, provided you don't mind months of writing, cooking, more writing, more cooking, testing, updating the writing, testing more, writing more, testing the writing, writing about the testing, quitting in a rage, rejoining in a sulk.

I love to cook and I somehow managed to pass that down to my daughter/co-author. Not just for the joy of creation, though that's wonderful (when it works—sometimes the joy of creation turns into "throw that away, don't even make eye contact with it"), but the expression on a loved one's face when you feed them something deliciously perfect, whether it's rose shortbread or a piece of fudge or a big fat muffin bursting with blueberries. They're hungry, you feed them something delicious. Then they're full *and* happy and don't whine as much. Theoretically.

There's a scene in *The Bear* where Sydney makes an omelet for her co-worker, Sugar. And it's a master class in why we cook for people we adore. Sydney's calm assurance, her attention to detail (cracking the eggs into a strainer, which catches the stringy albumen), her brisk whisking, the *whoosh* as she fires up the range, the generous pats of butter that sizzle. Her deft handling of the pan, the squeeze of the cheese down the center, more butter. Rolling the omelet onto the plate, another pat of butter rubbed on top. The addition of chopped chives and—genius—crumbled potato chips. It hits every button: creamy and crunchy and salty and bright and mellow. If you can watch that scene without drooling, you're probably a cyborg.

Sugar, exhausted and pregnant, devours it with relish: "This is so delicious I want to hug you."

That's it. That's why we cook. Because it's not just fuel. It's alchemy. It's showing you care by creating a literal example of affection and presenting it on a plate.

So I hope you use this book not just to make yourself happy, but the people you care about. If you make a batch of butterless chocolate chip cookies, your loved one will be gobbling a warm cookie within the hour. If you whip up some simple syrups and vanilla sugar, stick them in a shoebox, wrap the box in beautiful paper and slide it under their Christmas tree, you've helped someone you care about take care of themselves, too.

There's enough garbage in the world. Make something nice instead.

-- MaryJanice

Yet Another Introduction

This is the book that the entire CaFae Latte fanbase has been asking for since CaFae Latte became a *thing* back in February of 2023. As such, this is the book that I've been most nervous to write.

You want me to write a fantasy adventure? I can do that with my eyes closed.

World-build an entire society of mythological creatures and somehow make it work with the real world? With Google, I can do anything.

Write a recipe book? Eh…

It's not my specialty, is what I'm trying to say. I've been writing *stories* since elementary school, but only recently got the hang of even reading recipes. (Becoming an adult is honestly just figuring out which question to Google and following the instructions, hopefully without burning anything down.)

I don't enjoy cooking or baking as much as my mom does, and nobody is as good at cooking as their mother. It's the law.

But every now and then I get that itch to make something with my hands. Or, more often than not, I see a *really* good recipe on TikTok that I have to re-create (spoiler alert: that's how a lot of these recipes happened). And one thing I noticed early on is that it's much more satisfying to cook for other people in addition to yourself.

Mom mentioned the Dungeons and Dragons group in the dedication. Since they're at her house every week, it only made sense to have them test new recipes. There's a weird sense of nervousness when you cook for someone else—even if you've been friends forever, even if you've already tasted the dish and know that *you* like it, *they* might not. Especially with our D&D group, which includes a peanut allergy, a gluten allergy, a lactose allergy, and a vegetarian.

(Variety is the name of the game when it comes to feeding these people. Or anyone, really.)

But there's also a great sense of accomplishment when you get it right. Even when it's a tray of fudge you've been making since middle school, or a salad you whipped up in ten minutes. Something deeply primal gets scratched and satisfied when you make something physically sustaining for someone else.

As such, we've done our best to fill this book with a variety of recipes that are easy to make but also easy to *eat*. If you have a food allergy or avoidance, you should be able to either find something that won't kill you, and/or use a simple substitute.

That's really all I ask: don't make the food in this book the thing that kills you. That would *suck* for my first cookbook.

--Christina

Still Another Introduction

Naw, just kidding. That's it for the intros.

The Official CaFae Latte Cookbook

Written by Jennifer Charles Scott

With Commentary by Cyrus the Awesome!

Jennifer Charles' Introduction

"Make a cookbook," Bob said. "It'll be *fine*," she said. "It'll be an interesting side project."

Do you know how many times I've had to chase Cyrus out of the kitchen? How many *crappy* recipes get made for a single good one? How many times I accidentally used salt instead of sugar and so had to scrap the whole damn thing and start over?

More than once! On all of them!

But hey, if you guys want to suffer with me, I ain't stopping ya. You're probably not even reading this introduction. Who the hell reads the stuff *before* the recipes, anyway?

I'm Jennifer Charles, the kitchen manager and head baker of the insane asylum known as CaFae Latte. My qualifications? No one who's eaten my work has died from it, and only one keeled over from anaphylactic shock. (He had an epi pen, it was fine.)

Who the hell orders a pistachio chocolate chunk cookie when they're allergic to pistachios?

Idiots, Cyrus. Idiots do that.

Well, if you're going to die, I guess death by cookie is a pretty good way to go…

The CaFae uses a lot of magical ingredients which are hard to get and harder to work with, so for the purposes of this cookbook, we're keeping it simple with mundane stuff. No hellfire, no eldritch blood, no banshee tears. If you *want* to get those things, it's your funeral. Bob had to make a literal deal with Satan to get the hellfire alone, so good luck to you.

I pride myself on making a spread diverse enough that there's at least one thing for everyone, be they religious or allergic or whatever. I tried to put together a variety of recipes so that the gluten-free or dairy-free folks will have at least a few options that require little to no finagling. If the recipe calls for flour, you can usually use something like coconut or almond flour.

Just don't try to stab yourself with the cutting knife, and we'll get along great.

--JC

What You Need

Not much, I swear! Or at least, not much that you wouldn't ordinarily find lurking in your pantry or vegetable drawer or upstairs bathroom.

Pantry staples

All-purpose flour
(and/or the flour of your choice; coconut flour is my personal favorite gluten-free option)
Baking powder
Baking soda
Brown sugar, light or dark (I prefer light because molasses is nasty, and I love Splenda Brown)
Chocolate chips (whatever you like/need: ordinary, organic, dairy-free, etc.)
Chocolate (whatever you like/need: milk, dark, bittersweet, semisweet, etc.)
Cocoa powder (I like Ghiradelli or Guittard or Valrhona, but for those of us with a more realistic budget, Hershey's is fine)
Coconut milk(s)
Condensed milk(s)
Cooking spray
Corn starch
Herbs, dried (like thyme and rosemary)
Honey
Jam and/or jelly (unopened)
Kosher salt
Maple syrup
Nuts and nut butters of choice
Oats, rolled
Olive oil
Powdered sugar
Salt (whatever you love: sea, flakes, kosher, Himalayan, etc.)
Seeds (sunflower, etc.)

Spices, ground and whole (nutmeg, cinnamon, etc.)
Sugar (confectioner's, granulated, pearl, and/or your sweetener of choice...I love Splenda Blend)
Yeast
Vanilla beans
Vanilla extract (see the Syrups and Staples section on how to make your own)
Vanilla sugar (see above)
Vanilla salt (same)
Vegetable oil

Freezer

Fruit for smoothies
Butter
Margarine
Nuts of choice (they don't last long enough to go rancid in our house, but maybe not yours?)
Various dough (doughs?)

Fridge

Breads (I know, you're not supposed to refrigerate bread. But it's the only way to hold off the mold. Otherwise you've got blue bread in 48 hours.)
Butter
Cream
Eggs
Jam or jelly (opened)
Margarine
Milk(s) of choice

Equipment

Baking dishes, all sizes
Baking pans (9" x 13")
Baking sheets, ditto
Blender
Bowls (again, all sizes)
Cooling racks
Cutting boards
Jars, all sizes
Large spoons (wooden, silicon, etc.—good for whacking)
Loaf pan
Measuring cups
Mortar and pestle
Pastry brush
Saucepans
Silpats (silicone liners for cookie sheets—a Godsend!)
Spatulas (silicon, etc.)
Stand mixer
Teaspoon/tablespoon set
Whisks

Syrups and Staples

How Easy is That Vanilla Extract

I love vanilla and Ina Garten, the Barefoot Contessa, and never make me choose between them because there are no winners when you make me choose.

She's got a great recipe for homemade vanilla extract that I tried on a whim a few years ago and never went back. And it got me curious, so I did some research and apparently making your own extract has been a thing for several decades.

You can get high end vanilla extract at Williams-Sonoma for five hundred dollars (that's not an exact figure, but pretty much everything at Williams-Sonoma costs five hundred dollars). Or you can make your own for the cost of a few ounces of booze and 3-4 vanilla beans. And you'll never run out.

Ingredients:

- 3-4 vanilla beans (you can get them at most grocery stores, Amazon, or restaurant supply stores like Webstaurant)
- 8 ounces good vodka or rum (I prefer vodka)

Equipment:

- A jar (you don't even need a spoon for this one!)
- A sharp paring knife

Directions:

Slit your beans down the middle with your knife. This makes it easier for the vanilla pod to give up its lovely vanilla goodness. Then, depending on the length of your vanilla beans, stick them in your jar; if needs be, bend them or cut them in half so they fit. Fill your jar with vodka/rum.

Close it tightly and stick it in your pantry. Your vanilla extract is not yet vanilla extract; right now it's vanilla beans swimming in booze, the lucky bastards. Your jar needs to sit at room temperature for a month or so. *Then* you have vanilla extract. *La Contessa* advises you store it until "the beans are soft enough to cut the end and squeeze the seeds out". But I don't bother squeezing, and it's plenty vanilla-ey.

As it gets low, add more booze and beans as necessary. It'll keep in your pantry forever and ever.

I do a much smaller version, with 1 oz eye dropper bottles and 2 beans, and 2-3 eye droppers full is about a teaspoon, so I don't have to bother with measuring. That size bottle lasts me at least a month. Do what feels right and never look back.

Just as Easy Cinnamon Extract

The same concept, with cinnamon. It's nice to add to your baked goods, but it's even nicer for spicing up drinks. And chocolate! As with the vanilla extract, you can make a jar of this or, like me, just a few ounces.

Ingredients:

- 1-2 cinnamon sticks (Ceylon is best by far)
- 8 ounces good vodka or rum (I prefer vodka)

Equipment:

- A jar (you don't even need a spoon or knife for this one!)

Directions:

Put your sticks in your jar. Fill your jar with vodka/rum.

Close it and stick it in your pantry. Once your extract is as strong as you like it, remove the sticks. Unlike vanilla beans, if you keep cinnamon sticks in booze too long, your extract will turn bitter. And there's more than enough bitterness in the world.

Vanilla Sugar

I love keeping a cannister of this stuff on hand. It's easy to make, lasts forever, and gives off a wonderful perfume when you open the jar. And it makes a lovely gift.

Basically, all you're doing is letting your vanilla bean age in pure sugar, which is what they did before vanilla extract was a thing.

Ingredients:

- 2 cups granulated sugar (though you can make vanilla sugar out of brown, powdered/confectioner's, caster, pearl, sanding, cane, or turbinado sugar, and mixes like Splenda Blend)
- 1-2 vanilla beans (they're everywhere these days: grocery stores, spice stores like Penzey's, Webstaurant, Amazon, etc.)

Equipment:

- A jar (you don't even need a spoon!)

Directions:

Dump your sugar into your container of choice. Slit 1 or 2 of your vanilla beans down the middle; it releases seeds and aroma this way. Pop the whole beans into your sugar canister and push them most of the way down. Close it. Stick it in your pantry and ignore except when you need vanilla sugar. It's wonderful in tea, coffee, various baking recipes, over fruit...

How the fuck are you going to fill an entire recipe book with this bullshit? These aren't even recipes.

Shut up, Cyrus.

Cinnamon Sugar

As with vanilla sugar, this is easy to make and nice to have on hand.

Ingredients:

- 2 cups granulated sugar (though you can make cinnamon sugar out of brown, powdered/confectioner's, caster, pearl, sanding, cane, or turbinado sugars, or blends like Splenda Blend)
- 4 tablespoons ground cinnamon (I use Ceylon from Penzey's, but China works great, too)

Equipment:

- A jar (you don't need a spoon for this one, either)

Directions:

Dump your sugar and cinnamon into the container of choice. Seal. Shake. Pop it in your pantry. Done.

Vanilla Salt

Sounds weird, right? But think about all the dessert recipes that call for a pinch or half teaspoon of salt. The vanilla gives it that extra oomph. And who doesn't want more oomph?

Ingredients:

- 1 cup salt (You can use any kind, but I love Maldon salt flakes.)
- 1 vanilla bean

Equipment:

- A jar

Directions:

Slit your bean down the center, then dump the bean and the salt into your container of choice. Seal. Shake. Pop it in your pantry. Makes a wonderful if weird gift you'll have to explain. ("Think about all the dessert recipes that call for a pinch or half teaspoon of salt...")

Hey, so when are we going to get to the cooking and baking parts of the cookbook?

Simple Syrups

You can buy a bottle of simple syrup from Amazon for $14.99. Or you can make your own for about $0.70. This is so simple (thus the name!) it hardly needs a recipe. But here's one anyway.

Simple syrup is what happens when you dissolve equal parts sugar into hot water, then chill. It's wonderful in iced tea, coffee, cocktails...anytime you don't want to wait an hour for sugar to dissolve. It's also grand for making your own sparkling drinks.

Put some in a pretty jar with a cute ribbon, and you've got a nifty gift that doesn't blow up your bank account and is a practical-yet-luxurious addition to a kitchen.

Ingredients:

- 1 cup sugar
- 1 cup hot water

Equipment:

- Saucepan
- Spoon, preferably wooden
- Small clean mason jar(s) (avoid stealing it from your witch girlfriend's shelf; she'll be annoyed)

Directions:

Bring your water to a simmer.

Remove from heat, dump in your sugar. Stir until dissolved. If it looks cloudy, that's okay; just set it aside to cool. It'll clear up as it cools.

Once cool, pour into the container of your choice. It'll keep in the fridge for 2-3 months.

Variations:

As you're pouring sugar and water into your saucepan, pop a cinnamon stick in, too. Or a vanilla bean. Or crush a fistful of fresh mint or thyme or rosemary to release the oils, then drop them into your saucepan.

Once cooled, pour your syrup through a strainer into a bowl before pouring into jars. Label appropriately. Pat yourself on the back so hard you almost pull a muscle.

Beverages

Yarn Granny's Sweet Tea

You have no idea the things I had to do to get Yarn Granny's secrets of the Southern sweet tea. But there's nothing better on a hot day than sucking down something so sweet and refreshing it makes your teeth hurt and threatens an ice cream headache. And since the planet's being boiled alive via climate change, I think we deserve a cool, sweet treat.

You want to know the weirdest thing? Her whole family is made up of tea people. You go to her place, you're never going to find pop, but you'll find eighty different types of tea. "Pepsi?" "No, baby, we gave that up to stay healthy." "Ginger Ale?" "Nobody's been sick, so...no." "Root beer?" "*Not* in this house."

Ingredients:

- 5 cups water
- 6-7 black tea bags (I like Bigelow's Earl Grey or Constant Comment, and I like a strong tea, so I use at least 7 bags)
- 3/4 cup sugar (I know, it's a lot...but it's called Sweet tea, not Hmm This Could Use A Bit More Sugar tea)

Optional:
- ½ lemon, sliced, or a handful of fresh mint
- 1 pinch baking soda (it makes the tea clear, and Yarn Granny swears it's the secret ingredient)

Equipment:

- Tea kettle or saucepan for boiling water
- Long-handled spoon
- Pitcher

Directions:

Bring your water to boil. Once it's boiling, turn off your stove and add the tea bags. As above, I like a strong tea, so I steep for at least 15 minutes.

Slooooowly stir in your sugar, you're going to want to give it time to dissolve.

Yeah, even I, an avowed pig for sugar, don't like getting a mouthful of sugar granules that settled on the bottom of my glass and are taking their time dissolving.

If using, drop your pinch of baking soda into your empty pitcher. Take your tea bags out of the kettle and pour tea into your pitcher. Add ice until the pitcher is full. Add lemon slices and/or mint if you're inclined. Stir. Pop it in the fridge and chill until you want a nice big glass of sweet tea.

Serve in a mason jar with a slice of lemon if you're feeling precious. Serves 4.

Pucker Up Bitches Lemonade Stolen From Susan Branch

Ohhhhh, lemonade. One of those things that taste just as good when you're an adult as when you were a kid, unlike Happy Meals.

Speak for yourself.

Ingredients:

- ½ half gallon hot water
- ¼ cup water
- ¼ cup sugar
- 3 lemons
- 3 limes
- Zest of 1 lemon
- Zest of 1 lime

Equipment:

- Tea kettle or saucepan
- Smaller saucepan
- Medium bowl
- Long-handled spoon
- 6 cup pitcher

Directions:

Fill your kettle or saucepan with water and bring to a boil. Meanwhile, in your small saucepan, bring your ¼ cup of water to boil. Add ¼ cup sugar and stir until it's dissolved.

Add the zest of 1 lemon and 1 lime to your simple syrup. Add the juice of 3 lemons and 3 limes to your simple syrup.

Stir and pour into a 6-cup pitcher (or giant mason jar, or whatever you want to fill with lemonade). Chill for at least an hour; lemonade taste so much better when it's ice cold, unlike French fries.

Serve over ice and garnish with mint or basil or lemon basil. Serves 8. 6 if they're pigs.

Or just guzzle it down like you're in a contest and first prize is more lemonade!

Super Soothing Cider-ey Cider

The official CaFae Latte hot cider recipe is not just heated up cider in a mug. What the hell do you take us for? No, we steep it in a bunch of spices and top it with whipped cream.

Also, you can have cider cold, but if you prefer it that way, you're a weirdo.

Here's another recipe that almost doesn't need a recipe. Make it once, and you can make it forever after without looking it up.

Ingredients:

- ½ half gallon apple cider
- ¼ cup of caramel sauce, like Torani or Ghiradelli
- 2-3 cinnamon sticks
- 3-4 cloves
- 2-3 star anise

Optional:
- Teaspoon of nutmeg

Equipment:

- Medium saucepan or your slow cooker
- Long-handled spoon
- 6 cup pitcher

Directions:

Pop all your ingredients into your saucepan or slow cooker. If using the slow cooker, put it on high and your yummy hot cider will be ready in an hour.

If the saucepan, simmer your ingredients together over low heat for 7-8 minutes.

Pour into mugs, top with whipped cream and a sprinkle of nutmeg or cinnamon. Shove a cinnamon stick into the whip if you're feeling fancy. Drink. Done. Serves 6.

Delicious Flanders Cocoa

CaFae Latte has...feelings about hot chocolate. We like whole milk and really good chocolate and whipped cream and sprinkles, and sometimes a cookie nestled in the whip. We like Flanders' Cocoa: over the top and delicious, and the one thing we all agree on.

The Simpsons Movie **is a cinematic masterpiece, and the hot chocolate is partially responsible. Look at that pic and try, TRY not to drool.**

There's a reason Nicole gets our hot chocolate every day, even in summer.

Ingredients:

- 3 cups whole milk (or the milk of your choice, but the whole makes it decadent)
- Good hot chocolate mix, like Ghiradelli Hot Cocoa Mix, Cadbury Drinking Chocolate, Starbucks Hot Cocoa Classic, etc. Seriously, I know we've all got budgets and inflation's a bitch, but indulge in this one thing. Or you can make your own!
- 1 teaspoon cinnamon
- Pinch of salt (bust out your vanilla salt)
- Whipped cream
- Chocolate sprinkles or mini chocolate chips

Equipment:

- Whisk
- Saucepan or Hot Chocolate Maker (I've used the Nostalgia Retro Frother and Hot Chocolate Maker and the Mr. Coffee BMC-HC5 Café Cocoa Hot Chocolate Maker)
- Spoon

Directions:

Pour your milk into your saucepan and bring to a low simmer. Remove from heat, whisk in your chocolate, vanilla salt, and cinnamon until blended.

Alternatively, dump all your ingredients into your hot chocolate maker, turn it on, ignore it until it's done.

Pour into mugs. Top with whipped cream and sprinkles. Be resigned that your friends and family will never come to love any other kind of hot chocolate. If you make it for them once, you will make it for them until the day you die. Serves 3.

Delicious Flanders Cocoa Mix
(not that crap that comes in envelopes and goes in tepid water)

Sometimes you're short on time. Or money. Or both. So here's a mix that will deliver Flanders-esque goodness, provided you stir it into hot milk and not warm water like a sociopath.

Ingredients:

- ¾ cup unsweetened cocoa (the good stuff, like Ghiradelli or Guittard or Valrhona)
- ¾ cup sugar
- ½ teaspoon cinnamon
- Pinch of salt (this is a perfect time to bust out your vanilla salt)

Equipment:

- Whisk
- Medium bowl
- Spoon
- Jars

Directions:

Whisk it all together, pop it in your jar, stick jar in cupboard. Done. Then when you have a hankering, heat your milk and stir in 2 tablespoons (or to taste) until it melts. Top it with whatever decadence you desire.

Delicious Flanders Frozen Hot Chocolate

Hot chocolate is nearly always sublime, except when it's 95 degrees F (or 35 degrees in non-freedom units), when each time you venture outside if feels like you're breathing through a moist Ace bandage.

Enter frozen hot chocolate!

Ingredients:

- 2 tablespoons of your Delicious Flanders Cocoa Mix (or to taste)
- 1 cup ice
- 1 candy bar (I like Ghiradelli Milk Chocolate or Hersheys)

Equipment:

- Blender
- Spoon or silicone spatula

Directions:

Dump your DFCM, the ice, and the candy bar into your blender. Whir until it's a glorious blended mess. Pour into a glass. Top with whipped cream and sprinkles if you're inclined. Rejoice in the frozen goodness. Serves 1.

Dairy-Free Gluten-less Strawberry Smoothie

It's light, it's delish, it tastes like summer. And you can customize it just about any way you wish. Don't mind dairy? Use regular yogurt. Don't love strawberries? Weird, but okay...use blueberries or raspberries or melons. Want a lovely appetizer before whatever no-cook dinner you're having in the heat of summer? Pour it into a bowl and serve with spoons.

Ingredients:

- 1 cup dairy-free vanilla yogurt (fruit-based yogurts also work)
- 1/3 cup orange juice
- 2 pounds fresh strawberries, hulled and halved
- 1/4 cup sugar or honey

Equipment:

- Blender
- Spoon or silicone spatula
- Pitcher

Directions:

Dump it all in your blender and blend. Dump the contents of your blender into a pitcher. Refrigerate for at least 2 hours (it's much better cold). Sip. Smile. Serves 4.

For an extra bit of sweetness and crunch, top your serving with chocolate chips or sprinkles. Yeah, it undermines the whole point of a *healthy* drink/soup, but who cares?

Pumpkin Pie Smoothie

I came up with this for my friend, who would eat pumpkin pie at every meal if it was socially acceptable.

Is it not?

It's especially good in the fall, when it's not so cold the thought of frozen beverages makes you shudder. And like most smoothies, you can customize it. Swap out the yogurt and the milk for dairy-free options. Omit the milk. Add more milk. Go nuts.

Ingredients:

- ½ cup pumpkin puree
- 1 large banana
- 1-1/2 cup vanilla yogurt
- 1/3 cup whole milk (or the milk of your choice)
- ½ teaspoon pumpkin pie spice
- 8-10 ice cubes

Equipment:

- Blender
- Spoon or silicone spatula
- Pitcher

Directions:

Dump it all in your blender. Blend. Dump into a pitcher and/or glasses. Serves 2. Top with whipped cream and cinnamon if you wanna go fancy.

Iced Milk with Honey

I hate summer colds. All the gross inconvenience of a head cold—the snotty Kleenexes, the raspy-yet-nasal voice, the explosively gross sneezing—plus you've got to guzzle Nyquil when it's 90 degrees out. And you've got to drink hot tea or milk with honey, which is also annoying when you're sweating the tea out as fast as you can slurp it down.

Enter iced milk with honey! You'll actually stay hydrated while sick. Or even when you're not sick.

Ingredients:

- 3 cups milk of your choice
- 4 tablespoon honey
- 1 teaspoon cinnamon

Equipment:

- Saucepan
- Whisk
- Small spoon or rubber spatula
- Small pitcher
- ¼ measuring cup
- 1 cup measuring cup

Directions:

Measure your milk and pour into your saucepan over medium heat. You're not looking to boil it, you just want it to be receptive to honey. Ever dump honey into cold milk? Eeeuuggh.

Once your milk is steaming or very *very* lightly simmering, remove it from the heat and whisk in your honey. Here's a tip: if you spray your ¼ measuring cup with cooking spray, then add your honey, all that delicious sweetness pours right out without sticking. Bloop! It's weirdly satisfying.

Add your cinnamon, whisk more. Set aside to cool. Once cool, pour it into a pitcher and chill. Makes 3 small servings and is much nicer to drink than Nyquil.

Sweets

Gladiator Dates

This was blatantly stolen from the YouTube channel Tasting History, which did a video on what people would eat when visiting the Colosseum. Yes, *that* Colosseum, of Ancient Rome. Just like today's football stadiums, there were vendors where you could buy snacks while watching people kill each other. (And just like today's stadiums, they probably fleeced you for it.)

Stuffed dates were one of the more popular options, and it's obvious why. It's got a very unique blend of flavors, but man if they don't come together…

Ingredients:

- 1 dozen dates
- 1/3 cup sunflower seeds (or the nut of your choice; I usually go with a combination of almonds and cashews, although walnuts are the most traditional)
- 3/4 tablespoons honey
- 3 teaspoons salt
- 2 teaspoons black pepper

Equipment:

- Mortar and pestle or blender
- Saucepan
- Tongs
- Wooden spoon

Directions:

Slice your dates up one side for stuffing and pitting purposes. DO NOT cut all the way through. If they're already unpitted, then my hat is off to you, because I can never find the unpitted kind.

Mix your seeds and your black pepper in a blender, or use a mortar and pestle. (I may or may not steal my witch girlfriend's; you just need to clean it before putting it back.) You can smash them as much as you like, but I like leaving them at least partially whole so you get a nice crunch.

Stuff your dates with the seed/pepper mix. Hard. You want to jam as many seeds in there as you can. Then pinch your dates shut and roll them in the salt.

Pour your honey into your saucepan and simmer over medium-high heat for a good 10 minutes.

Add your dates to the honey with the cut side facing up. You want to ensure as few sunflower seeds escape as possible. Cook those l'il buggers for about a minute.

Take your dates out (carefully! yow! hot!) and place them on some sort of plate or platter. If you put tinfoil over it first, you'll save yourself a headache when doing the dishes later. Pop them in the fridge to cool for about an hour.

Normally this is where I would swoop in to steal a few, but they actually taste way better cold. I think it's a texture thing?

Serve. Gobble. Repeat. If any escaped your maw, put them back in your fridge, they'll keep for a couple of days. Y'know, in theory. They don't make it to midnight around here.

Fludge

Like smoke detectors, penicillin, and cheese puffs, Fludge was a mistake. It's what happens if you don't cook fudge long enough. It won't set, and you end up with a heavy, thick sauce that is wonderful over ice cream.

Or inhaled by the spoonful.

Ingredients:

- 2 cups sugar
- 1 stick butter
- 15 large marshmallows or 1-3/4 cup mini marshmallows
- 2/3 cup evaporated milk
- 1 teaspoon vanilla
- 8 oz chocolate chips

Equipment:

- Saucepan
- Spoon, preferably wooden (if you use a metal one, it'll get lava-hot)
- 8 x 8 pan, greased with butter or cooking spray

Directions:

Dump everything in a saucepan *except* the chips and vanilla and cook, stirring, at medium high heat until the mixture comes to a low boil. As everything starts to melt it will smell insanely good and you'll be tempted to sample.

You should give in to this powerful temptation, it's delicious. And you haven't even put in the chocolate chips yet!

Cyrus, stop writing in my cookbook or I'll lock you out of the kitchen.

Sorry.

But once the mixture is at a low boil, it will smell even better and you'll want to sample more. Don't! It's so hot at this stage, it'll burn your mouth. You'll spend the next 2 days with shredded skin on the roof of your mouth, which will make you grumpy, and you'll have to put up with multiple "I told you so's" by evil kitchen managers.

An-y-way, cook the whole bubbling mess at a low boil for 3-4 minutes. Once it's boiled long enough (you've got to stir constantly, too, did I mention that? yeah, stir like someone's holding you at knifepoint, or it'll burn and you'll ruin your pan and your kitchen will stink worse than usual), take it off the heat and dump in the chips and the vanilla.

Stir until the chips have melted. Now it'll smell really *really* good, but don't sample.

Again: *the pain, argh, my mouth, everything tastes like dead skin!*

Pour it into your greased 8 x 8 pan. Put it in the fridge to chill. Pour over ice cream, because ice cream by itself just isn't decadent enough.

Actual Fudge

If you want actual fudge, there's just a couple of extra steps.

Fair warning: this will ruin you for store-bought fudge.

Ingredients:

- 2 cups sugar
- 1 stick butter
- 15 large marshmallows or 1-3/4 mini marshmallows
- 2/3 cup evaporated milk (those mini-cans are *perfect*)
- 1 teaspoon vanilla
- 8 oz chocolate chips

Optional for Fairy Fudge:

- Edible dust and/or metallic/shiny sprinkles (carried by Etsy, Walmart, Amazon, Target, and most grocery stores). One little jar goes a long way.

Equipment:

- Saucepan
- Spoon, preferably wooden (if you use a metal one, it'll get hot, and if it's a plastic one, it'll melt which is bad for your spoon and it's not great for your fudge, either)
- 8 x 8 pan, greased with butter or cooking spray

Directions:

As with fludge, dump everything in a saucepan except the chips and vanilla and cook, stirring constantly, at medium high heat.

Cook the bubbling mess at a low boil for 5 minutes. Five! *At least five.* If you don't, you get Fludge, which is delicious, but not fudge. I sometimes cook it for 6-7 minutes to be safe.

Once it's cooked, take it off the heat and dump in the chips and the vanilla. Stir until the chips have melted, then pour it into your greased 8 x 8 pan. Add your edible dust and/or sprinkles. Chill. You'll know in an hour if you've got fudge or fludge. If it hasn't solidified by then, *it never will* and you'll have to face up to failure.

If it firms, dust with dust and/or cut it into squares and enjoy with a big glass of cold milk. You'll have about a dozen pieces, depending on how big you like your fudge squares.

Sugared Cranberries
Recipe I Definitely Didn't Steal From Pinterest

This is so easy, it barely needs a recipe. Make it once and you can make it always. Also, the pictures you will inevitably post look lovely and mouth-watering.

And the actual sugared berries will taste mouth-watering!

Personally I use them as decoration for other desserts, like tarts, but that's mostly due to the whole "trying to pass culinary school" thing. Academics like pretentiousness and high effort. Actual chefs and cooks prefer practicality and low effort.

Unlike, say, fudge, this recipe doesn't have to be exact. You can reduce or increase the sugar, cranberries, cinnamon sticks, etc. to taste.

Ingredients:

- 1 pound fresh cranberries*
- 3 cups sugar, separated: 2 cups, 1 cup
- 2 cups water

Equipment:

- Saucepan
- Spoon, preferably wooden (if you use a metal one, it'll get lava-hot)
- Container in which to dredge cranberries through snowy piles of sugar
- Parchment paper or tinfoil

Directions:

Make your simple syrup: combine the sugar and water in a saucepan and bring to a simmer.

Remove from heat and let cool for a bit (otherwise it'll cook some of your cranberries). After twenty minutes or so, dump the cranberries into the syrup and stir. Let them swim and bob in their sugar bath for at least 4 hours. (I stick the saucepan in the fridge and let it sit overnight. Raw cranberries are fantastically sour, so give them time to suck up syrup.)

Dump the last of your sugar, about a cup, on a plate or into a container of some sort. With a slotted spoon, remove the plump, syrup-infused cranberries from their delightful bath and roll them in the sugar a few at a time. Set them on a cookie sheet lined with parchment paper or tinfoil. (Warning: you will get sticky. I don't care if you're wearing a Hazmat suit; the sugar will get *everywhere*. Be resigned.)

You might need to add more sugar to the plate as the sugar starts to clump and isn't as eager to cling to the cranberries. Do not despair if it seems hard to get the sugar to stick to the berries. Everything will work out, I promise.

Let them sit out for an hour to dry—they'll get nice and crunchy and the sugar stays put. Once dry, you can put them in a pretty bowl or just unhinge your jaw and let them all tumble from the cookie sheet into your gaping maw.

Do not discard the cranberry-infused syrup, you maniac! Save it (I dump mine in mason jars) and stick it in the fridge. Now you've got cranberry-cinnamon simple syrup for iced tea. You can also save the leftover sugar on the plate for hot tea; who cares if it's crunchy and sticky? It's going in hot tea!

* Fresh cranberries are usually only available in November and December, depending on where you live. I like to buy extras and stash them in the freezer, because it's fun to see the look on guests' faces when they're presented with sugared cranberries in July.

Crazy Easy Chewy Chocolate Truffles a.k.a. Brigadeiros

These delicious fuckers got me my job at CaFae Latte. No joke: Bob put me on a trial run and I made brigadeiros and the customers loved them. The best part: they're so-so-sooooo easy. Are you sensing a theme in the recipes yet?

Get ready for the most chocolatey luscious bite-sized treat ever. Brigadeiros also come in flavors that aren't chocolate, but who cares?

Ingredients:

- 14 oz. sweetened condensed milk
- 2 tablespoon butter
- ¼ cup cocoa powder (for an extra-dark boost, use black cocoa like The Cocoa Trader, which gives Oreos that dark-dark black color)
- 1 cup sprinkles (chocolate is classic, but colored sugar gives it a nice crunch)

Equipment:

- Saucepan
- Wooden spoon

Directions:

Combine the cocoa, butter, and condensed milk in your pan and cook at low-to-medium heat. Don't be scared if it seems lumpy; that evens out. Stir *constantly*, because nothing is sadder or stinkier than burned chocolate.

When you can drag a rubber spatula across the bottom of your saucepan and see the bottom for 2-3 seconds before the chocolate surges back, it's ready.

Pour all the deliciousness onto a greased plate (I butter the plate, but you can use cooking spray if you prefer), and pop the plate in the fridge.

Chill *at least* an hour. If you don't, when you roll them into balls and through sprinkles and put them back, each Brigadeiro will flatten, so instead of a nice round ball you'll get an ungainly hockey puck.

After *at least* an hour, take out your plate. I often leave the plate overnight and roll my truffles in the morning.

Ooh, truffles for breakfast!

These aren't muffins, Cyrus. They're best as an afternoon snack.

So you've *never* had these for breakfast?

…anyway.

Pour your sprinkles onto another plate and butter your hands. Resist the temptation to nibble on your sweet buttery hands, *Cyrus*.

You ask me to help you in the kitchen, I will demand a reward!

With a cookie scoop, melon baller, spoon, or your fingers (though if you have long nails, it will take forever to get them clean), scoop up about a tablespoon of the chocolate and roll it into a ball an inch or so in diameter. Roll the ball through the sprinkles, and set aside. I pop them in a Tupperware container and place a paper towel between layers.

Chill and eat, then eat and chill.

Makes a dozen if you do it right, and half a dozen hockey pucks if you don't.

The hockey pucks still taste good, though.

Ooey Gooey Chocolate Oatmeal Bars

Sometimes, you can't (or won't) use your oven. Maybe it's broken. Maybe it's too hot. Maybe a magical salamander got in there and you have to wait for your dragon friend to get it out so you don't accidentally burn the whole place down.

Whatever the case, ovens aren't always an option, but you still want chocolate. Enter chocolate oatmeal bars.

Ingredients:

- 2-3/4 cup quick oats
- 1/3 cup peanut butter (or your substitute of choice)
- ½ cup honey, agave, or maple syrup (I used the latter—yum!)
- 1 tablespoon water
- ½ teaspoon salt (break out your vanilla salt)
- 1 teaspoon vanilla extract (and your homemade extract)
- 8 oz chocolate chips (or your chip of choice)
- ½ cup extra peanut butter

Equipment:

- 8 x 8 pan
- Cooking spray
- Parchment paper
- Microwave-safe small bowl
- Whisk or spatula or spoon

Directions:

Spray your 8×8 pan with cooking spray, then ignore it for now. Whisk your water, vanilla, maple syrup, and 1/3 cup peanut butter until smooth. Stir in the oats and salt.

Transfer about two-thirds of the mixture to your 8x8 pan. Press down hard; butter your hands or use a piece of parchment paper so you can really jam it down.

In your a separate bowl, carefully melt the chocolate and 1/2 cup peanut butter in your microwave in 30 second intervals. Stir, then pour on top of the oats you mashed into the pan. Sprinkle your remaining oats on top of the chocolate, then press down again.

Pop the whole thing into your fridge or freezer until firm enough to cut squares, about 2 hours for the fridge, 30 minutes for the freezer. Makes about a dozen squares.

Baked Goodies

Hellfire Mocha Cupcakes

CaFae Latte doesn't typically sell cupcakes (unless I lose a bet), but when we *do* sell them, these tend to be the bestsellers. The cakes are chocolate espresso with a bit of spice, so they're rich and moist and have the tiniest of kicks, while the frosting is vanilla with a hint of smoke.

I honestly don't know why we don't sell these full-time. Cupcakes are basically muffins with fancy hats.

They are *not*. They are two totally different foods, Cyrus.

Muffins are just bald cupcakes, and you know it!

They have completely different recipes and goals! Cupcakes are *cakes*. Light, fluffy, and always sweet. Muffins are dense and have the option to be savory.

Sounds like someone's just body-shaming the cupcake.

Keep talking like that and you won't get *any* cupcakes.

...I'll be good.

Also, fun fact: if the grocery store doesn't sell piping bags for frosting (yet sell piping *tips* for whatever reason), use a Ziploc bag. Preferably one of those hefty gallon-size ones that don't burst apart in your hands when you squeeze too hard and spray frosting all over the place.

This recipe makes about two dozen cupcakes.

Ingredients:

For the Cake:
- 1-3/4 cups flour
- 1 tablespoon flour
- 1-1/2 teaspoon baking soda
- 1-1/2 teaspoon baking powder
- 2 cups granulated sugar
- 3/4 cups unsweetened cocoa powder
- 2 large eggs
- 1/2 cup vegetable oil
- 1 cup room temperature milk of choice
- 3 teaspoons vanilla extract
- 1 cup espresso or brutally strong coffee, preferably fresh brewed and super-duper hot
- 1 teaspoon salt (great chance to use your vanilla salt!)
- 1 tablespoon cinnamon
- 1 tablespoon cardamom
- ½ tablespoon coriander (or more if you like it spicier)

For the Frosting:
- 5 cups powdered sugar (I know, it's a lot. But it's why buttercream frosting is so deliciously decadent)
- 4 sticks room temp unsalted butter
- 2 tablespoons vanilla
- 3/4 teaspoons liquid smoke

Optional:
- Food coloring (black for gray smoke effect, red for fire)
- Allllll the shiny sprinkles

Equipment:

- Large mixing bowl or stand mixer
- Rubber/silicone spatula
- Cupcake sheet
- Cupcake liners if that's how you wanna go

Directions:

Preheat your oven to 350 degrees Fahrenheit, making sure there's a rack in the center.

Add sugar to a mixing bowl of a stand mixer (or just do it by hand if you don't want to clean the mixer later). Add the flour, cocoa powder, baking soda, baking powder, salt, cinnamon, cardamom, and coriander into the sugar bowl. Ideally you'd have a paddle attachment, but use what you got. Mix for about 30 seconds until it's the same color. Set aside.

In a small bowl, whisk the eggs, oil, milk and vanilla until it's *almost* completely combined. Add this mixture to the sugar/flour mixture of the stand mixer bowl. Mix the ingredients on low until it's all *just* incorporated, about 30 seconds.

With mixer off, pour in the espresso/hot coffee. Mix by hand, scraping down the bottom of the bowl to get all the batter incorporated. A few lumps are ok. The batter will be *very* runny. Let it rest for 5 minutes.

The runniness makes this batter less than ideal when licking the bowl and spatula, but it's still pretty good.

Line a standard muffin tin or cupcake pan with cupcake cups. Fill each cup with batter to about 3/4 full, about 3 tablespoons each.

Bake cupcakes for 22-24 minutes. The cupcakes are done when they pass the toothpick test.

LET THE CUPCAKES COOL COMPLETELY BEFORE ADDING FROSTING. Otherwise, the icing will melt and create a pool of liquid icing all over the counter.

For the frosting:

Put butter in a mixing bowl (either regular or with your stand mixer). Use your mixer to cream the butter until it's fluffy, about 5 minutes. Again, you'll ideally have a paddle attachment and not the more common beater or whisk, because otherwise you're going to have to stop every other minute to poke the butter out from between the metal so it actually *mixes*. But again, use what you got.

Gradually add the powdered sugar a little at a time, waiting until it's incorporated to add more. Otherwise, sugar's going to go *everywhere*.

Once the frosting is completely mixed, add the vanilla and liquid smoke. Be *very careful* with the liquid smoke; a little goes a very long way. If you're adding food coloring, do it here. Mix until incorporated.

Put the frosting in the piping bag (or Ziploc) and pipe onto the cupcakes—again, AFTER THEY'RE COMPLETELY COOL.

Once each cupcake is frosted, add sprinkles. I typically go with red on gray frosting, because hellfire.

Big Fat Buttery Blueberry Scones

Thus called because they're just big fat buttery blueberry scones. It's like a tender, blueberry-studded brick you can eat.

Scones are yet another baked good I assumed was difficult to make unless you had a Diplôme de Pâtisserie hanging in your bathroom. But I was wrong, as I have been so very, very often in my life; they're easy and you feel like a real baker when you take them out of the oven and ponder where you'll hide them so you actually *get to eat one this time.*

Gotta be quicker, JC.

Ingredients:

- 2-1/2 cup flour
- ½ cup sugar (I use my granulated vanilla)
- 2-1/4 teaspoon baking powder
- 2 tablespoon sugar (it's to add some sparkle and crunch to the top of your scones; I use turbinado, but sparkling sugar, Sugar in the Raw, etc. work just fine)
- 1 cup blueberries
- 1 egg
- ¾ cup milk (I use whole milk which is positively stuffed with dairy; you do you)
- ½ cup cold butter (whatever you've got on hand)

Equipment:

- Box grater

- Medium/Large mixing bowl
- Rubber/silicone spatula or wooden spoon
- Cookie sheet

Directions:

Take your chilled butter and grate it with your box cutter. It's weird but doesn't take long, so shut up and do it. Store your shredded butter in the freezer, then get back to work.

Dump your sugar, salt, baking powder, and flour into your medium or large mixing bowl; stir or whisk to combine.

Now you'll add your shreds of butter to the dry ingredients, then mix or toss. I just use my hands.

Add your milk and egg and combine with your spoon and spatula. Your dough will be super thick, so you'll have to finish mixing with your hands, anyway. You want your flour completely incorporated.

Add your blueberries and caaaaarefully mix in. If you mash like a maniac, you'll mush them all up.

Sad. No one wants mushy blueberries.

Now pop your dough in the fridge for 2 hours. (I said the recipe was easy. Not quick.)

When you're ready to bake, preheat your oven to 400 degrees Fahrenheit. Take your dough out of the fridge, sprinkle some flour on your cutting board or counter, and roll the sconey-goodness into a circle with a rolling pin. You can also use your hands if you like the rustic look. You want your dough to be between ½ and ¾ of an inch thick.

Slice your disc of dough into 8 triangles. Sprinkle them with your sparkle or turbinado sugar.

Pop them in the oven for 20 minutes. They're done when the tops are light golden brown. Remove from oven. Let cool. Cower when your coworkers hear the oven timer and thunder into the kitchen to help themselves like a pack of wolverines. Fight them off with the rolling pin if necessary, so at least *something* gets to the customers.

They'll keep for 3 days. Theoretically.

Dragonfire Muffins

Sometimes you don't want something super-sweet. You're leaning more toward savory, maybe even with a little danger in your muffin. Angst, even. And also spices.

Dragonfire muffins are spicy blackbread muffins, best eaten hot with a bit of butter on top. Pop them in the microwave to re-heat if you need to; it's way better than having them cold.

Ingredients:

- ¼ cup light or dark brown sugar
- 1 cup flour (I recommend using coconut flour if you need it gluten-free)
- ½ cup dark rye flour (rice flour for gluten-free)
- ½ cup medium-grind cornmeal (which is naturally gluten-free)
- 1 teaspoon cayenne pepper
- 1 teaspoon cinnamon
- 2 teaspoons unsweetened cocoa powder
- 1-1/2 teaspoons baking soda
- ¾ teaspoon salt (I use Maldon smoked sea salt for this)
- 4 tablespoons unsalted butter, which you'll melt and let cool
- 1/3 cup molasses (or maple syrup if you're a heathen)
- ¼ cup vegetable oil
- 1 egg
- ¾ cup buttermilk*

Optional:

- ¾ cup raisins or sunflower seeds

Equipment:

- Large bowl
- Small bowl
- Wire rack
- Rubber or silicone spatula
- Whisk or spoon
- Muffin tin
- Muffin tin liners (if using)

Directions:

Preheat your oven to 400 degrees F. Take your muffin tin and spray with your cooking spray. You could also line each muffin slot with paper or silicone liners instead. Set aside; its time will come.

In your large bowl, combine your cocoa powder, cornmeal, the flours, baking soda, and salt; stir.

In your medium bowl, add your brown sugar, oil, your melted butter, and the molasses. Stir to combine. Then add your buttermilk and egg, stir.

Add your wet mixture to your dry, folding with your spatula until *just* mixed, with no dry spots. Don't overmix, or it will be like eating a delicious hockey puck. Unless that's your thing, in which case, overmix with abandon.

Fold in your raisins/sunflower seeds if you're using them, then scoop your batter into your muffin tin. You want each tin about ¾ full.

Bake for 12 minutes on a rack in the center of your oven, or when a toothpick comes out clean. Let cool until you can eat them without pain. Serve with room-temp butter. Marvel at your skills.

* No buttermilk on hand? Lactose-intolerant? You can make some: add a tablespoon of vinegar or lemon juice to a cup of milk (can be regular or dairy-free). Stir gently, let sit for about 5 minutes. It'll be clumpy; that's what you want.

Grammy's Andes Mint Cookies

These are the taste of Christmas; my late grandmother made them every year. You can make them any time of the year, but I stick to the holidays. They look great, too, like they were hard to make, and they aren't. But be warned: this is not a "let's go in the kitchen and whip these up recipe." You'll need to give the dough time to chill.

Ingredients:

- 2-3/4 cups flour
- 1-1/2 cups brown sugar
- ¾ cup butter (1-1/2 sticks)
- 2 eggs
- 12 oz chocolate chips
- ½ teaspoon salt
- 1-1/4 teaspoons baking soda
- 2 tablespoons water
- 24 Andes mints

Equipment:

- Saucepan
- Wooden spoon
- Cookie sheet
- Offset spatula or small spoon

Directions:

Melt your butter in a saucepan over medium heat. Add the brown sugar and water, stirring occasionally.

Add the chocolate chips and stir until they're melted, too.

Remove from heat and let the mixture stand 10 minutes.

Add your remaining ingredients—the eggs, flour, salt, and baking soda—and combine to form the dough. The dough's a bit heavy, so I use a hand mixer for this part.

Put your saucepan in the fridge and chill the dough at least an hour. I often make the dough in the evening and chill it overnight because Cyrus doesn't come into the kitchen after hours.

Once chilled, preheat your oven to 350 degrees F and strip the paper off all your Andes mints. (I usually make Drek do it. If I enlist Cyrus, half of those mints mysteriously disappear.)

The digestive system *is* a mystery. Medical research really should be better funded, you know.

With a cookie dough scoop or spoon, scoop your dough and roll them into balls. Put them on a cookie sheet, leaving room to spread. I do 3 balls, 2 balls, 3 balls, 2 balls per sheet.

Pop those l'il suckers into your oven for 8 to 9 minutes.

When you take them out, place an Andes mint on each cookie at once. I've heard of versions of this recipe that call for splitting the mints in half and just putting half a mint on each cookie and I tell you without hyperbole *that way is bullshit.*

Wait 2-3 minutes for the mint to melt, then swirl it with an offset spatula or the back of a spoon.

Let cool, and don't stack them until they're all the way cool or you'll just have a mess. Happy holidays! Or Easter, or whenever you're making them.

Eggless Shortbread Chock Full o'Roses

Don't tell the Wulver that we're stealing from his homeland.

Shortbread is a traditional Scottish cookie ("biscuit", if you will, and I will) and the basic formula hasn't changed much in 300 years: 1 part sugar, 2 parts butter, 3 parts flour. Mix. Bake. Magic. If you're Jewish and use kosher flour, you can have it over your holidays, too. (Guess what Rethu got as a little Passover present?)

It's easy to switch it up, too, when you add stuff like rose water and/or dried rose petals. And the varieties are endless. Not a fan of roses? Lavender's nifty. So is thyme. Try cinnamon or chocolate. Shortbread is also lovely topped with sugared flowers like pansies.

Go wild! The only limitations are in your mind. Or your fridge. And probably your budget.

Ingredients:

- 2 cups flour
- 1 cup granulated sugar
- ¾ cup softened (room temp) butter (1-1/2 sticks)
- 1-1/4 teaspoons baking soda
- 2 teaspoons rosewater (or lavender water, or orange blossom water, or...)
- 2 tablespoons dried rose petals

Equipment:

- Medium bowl
- Rubber/silicone spatula

- Cookie sheet, preferably with a Silpat

Directions:

In your bowl, beat the butter and sugar until it's light and fluffy.

Add your rosewater (or whatever floral water you're using), beat for a minute or so.

Add your flour, baking soda, and dried rose petals. You can smash the roses in your fist or a mortar and pestle if you like so you've got smaller pieces.

Bring it all together into a dough with your spatula, or your hands if it doesn't seem like it wants to come together. If it remains recalcitrant, add 1 or 2 tablespoons of milk.

Your dough, once you've brought it to heel, should be nice and soft.

Divide it in half, and roll each half into a log or a rectangle, whichever you like.

Put your logs on your baking sheet, and pop it in the fridge for half an hour or so.

When it's time to bake, preheat your oven to 355 degrees F.

Take your logs out of the fridge and slice them up. I've seen recipes suggest you cut them about 1/8" thick, but that's too thin for me. I'm not after a sweet cracker, I want a proper cookie. So I cut them about half an inch. You do you.

Bake for 8-10 minutes or until your shortbread is a nice light golden color.

Pull them out of the oven and let cool for 5 minutes or so before transferring to a cooking rack. Don't fret, they'll get firmer as they cool.

Store in a jar or Ziploc bag or Tupperware or what-have-you. You'll have a lightly sweetened chewy cookie with a lovely rose perfume.

Grammy's Extra-Crummy Apple Crumble

Everyone knows that the crumb and crumble is better than the apple or pear beneath. My late grandmother's recipe reflects that: 1/3 fruit, 2/3 delicious crumbly topping. You can substitute any fruit you like, or combine them. Apple/pear is especially good.

Ingredients:

Fruit:
- 4-5 apples; I've made this with all kinds of varieties— Gala, Golden Delicious, Honeycrisp, Red Delicious— and they all come out fine. Buy whatever's local and/or on sale.
- Sugar, cinnamon, and nutmeg to taste

Crummy Crumble:
- 1 stick room temperature unsalted butter (no biggie if you only have salted on hand)
- 1 stick room temp margarine (I never have margarine so I always use 2 sticks of butter...again, a matter of taste)
- 2 cups flour
- ¾ cup granulated sugar
- ¾ cup brown sugar

Equipment:

- Medium-sized bowl to hold the apples and, later, the crummy crumble
- Spoon
- 9" x 13" baking pan

Directions:

Pre-heat your oven to 375 F. Butter, grease, or spray your 9" x 13" pan and set aside.

Peel, core, and slice your apples. I leave the peel on for extra fiber, but take it off if you just fucking hate fiber, or need to keep a certain fairy at bay.

Dip the peels in honey, and it's a much more socially acceptable way to eat honey by the spoonful.

Toss sliced apples with sugar, cinnamon, and nutmeg to taste. I use 1 tablespoon granulated sugar and 1 teaspoon each of cinnamon and nutmeg. You can skip this step if you're not a pig for sugar like Cyrus.

Or if you're weak.

Dump your apples into your greased baking pan. In the now-empty bowl, mix the margarine, butter (you can slice up your butter into tablespoons first if that's easier), flour, and sugars. Use a pastry cutter, a big fork, or your hands to mix it all together until it's nice and crumbly.

Dump your crummy crumble over your apples. It's okay if it looks like a big old mess. That's what you want: a mess! Pop your pan in the oven and bake for 40-45 minutes, until top is golden and apples are soft enough to pierce with a toothpick or fork.

Let it cool, but not too long. It'll never taste better than when it's still warm from the oven. Serve with a scoop of vanilla ice cream for some real decadence.

Butterless Chocolate Chip Cookies

I can't tell you how often I've decided to make cookies only to find I'm either out of butter or only have frozen butter (most recipes call for room-temp). Or I'm out of flour. Or chocolate chips. Or eggs. Or everything. This recipe will solve one of those problems; you can whip them up and you don't have to chill the dough. In less than an hour you've got warm cookies to present to guests.

These thin, chewy cookies spread as they bake. Drop smaller, fatter rounds of dough, they end up thick and chewy. It's legit impossible to tell these cookies apart from the buttery versions.

Ingredients:

- 2-1/2 cups flour
- 1½ teaspoon salt (break out your vanilla salt!)
- 1½ teaspoon baking powder
- 1 teaspoon baking soda
- 11-1/4 cup brown sugar
- ½ cup white sugar
- 2 eggs
- 2 cups chocolate chips (whatever kind floats your boat)
- ¾ cup vegetable oil
- 1 teaspoon vanilla

Equipment:

- Medium bowl
- Mixer
- Rubber/silicone spatula
- Cookie dough scoop
- Cookie sheet
- Wire rack

Directions:

Preheat your oven to 350 degrees F.

Mix your flour, baking powder, baking soda, and salt in your medium bowl. Set aside.

In your stand mixer, combine the oil with the brown and white sugars. Add your eggs one at a time, and follow up with your vanilla.

Add your dry ingredients and, when mixed, the chocolate chips. Mix until evenly combined.

Scoop balls of dough and drop them on your cookie sheet (lined with a Silpat or cooking spray) about 2 inches apart.

Bake for 8 to 9 minutes. Remove from oven (duh), and let them cool before moving them onto your wire rack.

Smooooky Brownies

Every family has their own lexicon. My brother called the waterpark's Jacuzzi the Magoozi until he was in middle school. When I was little, I mispronounced the Galapagos Islands as Guh-*lack*-uh-pose, and now the whole family does it. I had to look up the actual pronunciation so I could spell it the right way for this recipe, because children are a pain in the ass.

Also when my sister was very small, things weren't spooky, they were smooky. Which, honestly, sounds better. Smookier, as it were.

Anyway, here's a recipe for brownies that look like mummies. We sell them at CaFae Latte for Smooky Season.

Ingredients for the brownies:

- ½ cup cocoa powder
- ½ cup sugar
- ½ cup brown sugar (light or dark to taste)
- 1/2 cup flour
- Pinch of salt (like your vanilla salt!)
- ½ teaspoon baking powder
- 2 eggs
- ½ cup/1 stick cooled, melted butter (I microwave mine, then pop it in the fridge for 15 minutes or so)
- 1 teaspoon vanilla extract (see Syrups and Staples for how to make your own)
- ½ tablespoon instant coffee or espresso powder
- Cooking spray

Ingredients for the frosting:

- 1 cup powdered sugar
- ¼ cup butter/half a stick room temperature, unsalted
- 1/2 teaspoon vanilla extract (see Syrups and Staples for how to make your own)
- Pinch of salt (see above: vanilla salt!)
- Teeny candy eyeballs (I said they were *smooky* brownies, didn't I?)

Equipment:

- 8 x 8 baking pan (you'll end up with about a dozen brownies)
- 2 medium bowls
- Stand mixer or hand mixer
- Parchment paper
- Rubber/silicone spatula

Directions:

Pre-heat your oven to 350 degrees F. Spray your 8" x 8" pan with cooking spray, then line with parchment paper. I know...it's a pain in the ass. But it's the best way to lift your brownies out for cutting and frosting.

In one of your mixing bowls, combine your sugars, baking powder, vanilla salt, cocoa, and flour. Whisk and set aside.

In your other bowl, crack your eggs and whisk, then add your vanilla and your cool butter.

Add your wet ingredients to your dry and stir. Spread into your parchment paper-prepped pan. Bake for 25 minutes, or until a toothpick comes out clean. Be careful not to overbake.

Let cool completely. NEVER TRY TO FROST A WARM BROWNIE/CAKE/ETC. The frosting will just melt and make a mess.

Still tastes good, though.

While your brownies are cooling, make your frosting: whip your butter in your other bowl until smooth. Add your vanilla and/or vanilla salt, mix until well incorporated.

Slooooowly add the powdered sugar a little bit at a time, until incorporated completely. Careful! It poofs up into a cloud if you go too fast. Beat until your frosting is nice and smooth. If it seems a little crumbly, add about a tablespoon of the milk of your choice.

So far they're just brownies; here's how to make them smooky:

Fit a large piping bag with something called a coupler, use the flat tip, fill with frosting. No bag? No problem; a gallon-sized Ziploc also works.

Carefully grasp your parchment paper and gently lift the brownies out of the baking pan.

Cut the giant brownie into 12 smaller brownies.

Use your piping tip to run random strips of icing back and forth. Stick 2 candy eyes to each brownie. Or more, if you want.

Enjoy allllll the smookiness.

S'mores Banana Bread

I never bought into the whole "It's got bananas in it, it's good for you!" misinformation. Chocolate-covered bananas also have bananas in them, but c'mon. No one's going to mistake a monkey tail for a salad.

That said, this recipe isn't entirely bad for you. And it's easy! Warning: if you make it, there's a risk you'll crave *actual* s'mores, and then find yourself roasting marshmallows over your gas stove while your girlfriend watches and questions all her life choices.

Ingredients:

- 1 cup chocolate chips of choice
- 1 cup coarsely broken graham crackers (about 4 crackers)
- 1 cup baby marshmallows
- 1 teaspoon baking powder
- ½ teaspoon baking soda
- 1-1/2 cups flour
- ½ cup unsweetened cocoa powder
- ½ teaspoon salt (vanilla salt!)
- ½ cup vegetable oil
- 2 eggs, beaten
- 1-1/2 cups smooshed super-ripe banana (about 4)
- ½ cup granulated sugar
- ½ cup brown sugar, packed
- 1 teaspoon vanilla
- Cooking spray

Equipment:

- 1 small mixing bowl
- 2 medium mixing bowls
- Rubber or silicone spatula
- 9 x 5 inch loaf pan
- Wire rack

Directions:

Preheat your oven to 350 Fahrenheit. Grease or spray your bottom. Um, the bottom of your 9 x 5 inch loaf pan, I mean. The bottom and an inch or so up the sides.

Combine your baking powder, baking soda, salt (or vanilla salt), flour, and cocoa powder. Then make a little well in the center.

Grab your medium bowl and combine your eggs (pre-beat!), banana, both sugars, vanilla, and your vegetable oil. Dump that into the well of your dry mix. Stir until *just* moist. Then fold in ¾ cup of your chips, graham crackers, and marshmallows.

Pour your batter into your greasy loaf pan.

In a small bowl, combine what's left of your chips, crackers, and marshmallows; sprinkle them over your batter.

Bake for 55-57 minutes or when your toothpick emerges squeaky-clean. You might need to cover the top with foil in the last 15 minutes or so to prevent the marshmallows from over-browning. When I'm making actual s'mores, I burn the holy shit out of the marshmallow and devour it while it's black and blistered.

That ruins the marshmallow! You want it *just* cooked enough that the outsides start to get brown and crunchy, leaving the inside gooey and squishy for the perfect s'more texture.

Whatever. You do you.

Cool on your wire rack for ten minutes or so. Then pop it out of your loaf pan and finish cooling. You'll get about 6 slices if you're a black hole like Cyrus, and 8 if you're a normal person. It'll keep in your fridge for 3-4 days.

Rosemary Focccccacccccia
(I can never remember all the C's in Focaccia)

If you think making your own bread is too hard or just a big fat waste of time, this is the recipe to try. Year ago, I got hooked on no-knead Dutch oven artisan bread, the sort of recipe you find is easy and yields wonderful results and you're kicking yourself for not discovering it a decade earlier.

The no-knead Dutch oven bread was my gateway bread. I didn't know I even liked Foccccccacia until I made it; now I'm hooked. Letting the dough rise takes a couple of hours, but said dough comes together fast and easy, and what comes out of the oven is crispy-on-the-outside, tender on the inside Focacia. My advice is to eat it fast, before the rest of your coworkers find out there's fresh-baked focacccccia in the kitchen.

Ingredients:

- 4 cups flour, separated into 3 cups and 1 cup
- ¼ cup olive oil
- 1-1/2 cups warm water (tap water will do, anything in the area of 120 degrees F to 130 degrees F)
- 1 teaspoon active dry yeast
- 3 teaspoon kosher salt, separated into 1/2 teaspoon and 1/2 teaspoon
- Cooking spray
- 1 tablespoon fresh rosemary, finely chopped (if you're not a fan of rosemary, thyme works beautifully, and so does nothing)

Equipment:

- Large bowl
- Measuring spoons
- Long-handled spoon
- 15 x 10 inch baking pan (I don't have one; I use a small cookie sheet and spread the dough all the way to the end...works great!)
- Plastic wrap, the bane of my existence

Directions:

Combine the 3 cups of flour, yeast, and ½ teaspoon salt in your bowl, and mix with your long-handled spoon.

Add your warm water and stir the dough with the end of your spoon until it comes together. The dough will be mildly gross, all soft and sticky.

Cover your bowl loosely with horrible plastic wrap which is tough to get off the roll and bunches up like crazy and sometimes you can't find the loose part because it's stuck to the roll and it's just a pain in the ass, *God*, I hate cling film. It's a battle every time. But sometimes it's the only thing that will do, dammit.

Anyway, let that rest for 2 hours. Breathe. Resist the urge to cling film yourself into unconsciousness.

Your dough should be much bigger than when you started, all jiggly and puffy. So pour about a tablespoon of olive oil into your pan and spread it to and up the edges of the pan with a pastry brush (you can also use a paper towel).

Here's where you add that last cup of flour to the dough in the bowl, stirring with the handle of your wooden spoon until incorporated.

Why the handle?

The dough is *really* sticky, and if you use the spoon side, you'll end up with half the dough stuck to it. Alternatively, you can try spraying the spoon with cooking spray.

Then you'll dump your dough into your prepared baking pan and gently spread it out until it reaches each corner.

Take another strip of awful, *awful* Saran Wrap, apply cooking spray to one side, then lay it spray-side down on your dough. This covers the dough without letting it stick to the wrap. Let rest for 90 minutes.

Preheat your oven to 400 degrees F. When it's ready, remove your nasty plastic wrap, then poke holes all over your focacccccccia dough with your fingertips, drizzle 2 tablespoons of olive oil over it, and sprinkle with the remaining ½ teaspoon salt.

Bake for 30 minutes, until golden brown. It will never taste better than the day it's made, so waste no time devouring all the foccccccacia goodness.

Done and done!

Chocolate Chunk Pistachio Cookies

Pistachios in dessert is one of those dividing lines among people. Some love it, others think it's nuts. (Heh.) This is the recipe that will convert the non-believers.

If you're allergic to pistachios, just nix them, and you've got really good chocolate chunk cookies.

Ingredients:

- 1 cup butter, room temperature
- ¾ cup brown sugar
- ½ cup granulated sugar
- 2-3/4 cups flour
- 2 large eggs
- 2 teaspoons vanilla extract
- 1-1/4 cups unsalted or raw pistachios, coarsely chopped
- 1 cup semi-sweet chocolate chips
- 4 oz semi-sweet chocolate, cut into pieces (or bagged chocolate chunks)
- 1-1/2 teaspoon baking powder
- ¼ teaspoon baking soda
- 1 tablespoon corn starch
- ¼ teaspoon salt (perfect time to use your vanilla salt!)

Equipment:
- Medium bowl
- Large bowl
- Whisk

Directions:

Preheat your oven to 350 degrees Fahrenheit.

In a medium bowl, whisk your flour, baking powder, baking soda, corn starch, and salt; set aside.

In a bigger bowl (or your stand mixer bowl) add your butter, brown sugar, and granulated sugar. Beat until creamy. Add your eggs one and a time and beat until smooth; add your vanilla.

Pour your dry mixture into your wet; stir until combined. Dump in half of the chocolate pieces/chunks and the pistachios, and the chocolate chips. Stir until *just* incorporated; remember my dire warnings about overmixing.

Using an ice cream scoop (whatever you've got on hand should be fine), scoop your dough onto your cookie sheet. Press extra chocolate chunks on top of the balls of dough. Cover your balls (heh) with the hated plastic wrap and pop it into the fridge while your oven preheats.

Remove your balls from the fridge and place 5-6 balls of dough on your cookie sheet. You'll need at least 2 inches between each ball.

Bake 13-15 minutes; watch carefully and don't overbake! Remove from oven (duh...seems like unnecessary instruction) and add more chocolate chunks to each cookie, as many as you can cram on there. Let cool 10-15 minutes. These are great warm, but even better the next day.

Cracker Crack

O holiest of holies, these are sooooo good. And sooooo bad for you.

A true pantry snack, since there are just a few ingredients and chances are you've got them on hand. This recipe also works great when you've got partial bags of chocolate, butterscotch, dark, white, or whatever kind of chips on hand. You can clean out your pantry *and* make yourself a delicious treat. This recipe is also easily halved.

Ingredients:

- 48 saltines
- 2 sticks butter/margarine
- 2/3 cup granulated sugar
- 3 cups chocolate chips (or your chip of choice)
- 1 teaspoon vanilla

Equipment:

- Cookie sheet
- Tinfoil
- Microwave-safe small bowl
- Offset spatula or spoon

Directions:

Preheat your oven to 350 degrees F. Then line your cookie sheet with tinfoil, making sure there are no gaps. Double-line if you must. Since it's not Saran Wrap, it should cooperate and you won't scream and scream in frustration.

Meanwhile, melt your butter and sugar in the microwave (you can also use your stovetop). While it's melting, lay out your crackers onto your cookie sheet, side by side. Don't overlap but make sure they're all touching.

Add vanilla to your butter/sugar mixture, stir. Then pour your mixture evenly over your crackers. Use your offset spatula to make sure all the crackers are covered. If you see gaps, ease the crackers back together. Then pop the whole thing in your oven for 7 minutes.

No refrigeration?

Nope, there's no window for your theft, Cyrus.

Aw...

When time's up, take out your cookie sheet and evenly sprinkle your chocolate chips over the crackers. Move one of your oven racks to the top, and pop your sheet back in for 2 minutes, then take them out again.

Spread the melted chips evenly over your crackers with a spatula or back of a spoon. Let the whole mess cool for 30 minutes, then pop it, cookie sheet and all, into your freezer for at least 3 hours or overnight.

When you want to chow down, peel the tinfoil off the back of the crackers and break your snack up into smaller pieces. I like to keep them in a Ziplok bag in the freezer. I also like not telling anyone they're in there, which ensures I'll get some. Savages. I'm surrounded by savages.

The Corniest of all the Bread(s)

I'm writing this just as the weather is obliging us with milder temps and gorgeous red leaves, when it's too cool for iced coffee but too warm for hot chocolate (if you aren't a Buddhist witch named Nicole, anyway).

Enter cornbread, which is satisfyingly light but you still feel like you ate something (not like meringue, that faker). Plus, so easy! People are always impressed when you whip out a loaf. Don't tell 'em it only took about half an hour, including baking time.

Ingredients:

- ½ cup flour
- ½ cup cornmeal (yellow, white, or blue)
- ¼ cup melted butter
- 1 large egg yolk (no white; feed it to your dog for their shiny coat)
- ½ cup buttermilk
- ¼ cup brown sugar
- ¼ teaspoon salt (use your vanilla salt!)
- ¼ teaspoon baking powder
- ¼ teaspoon baking soda
- 2 tablespoons honey

Equipment:

- 8.5" x 4.5" loaf pan
- Cooking spray
- Microwave-safe small bowl
- 1 medium bowl
- Whisk or spatula or spoon

Directions:

Preheat your oven to 400 Fahrenheit. Spray your loaf pan with cooking spray, then ignore it for now.

Melt your butter in your small bowl in the microwave; 90 seconds or so for already-softened butter should be fine. Longer for refrigerated or frozen butter, obviously.

In your medium bowl, mix your dry ingredients: your cornmeal, flour, baking soda, baking powder, and salt.

Grab your other bowl and whisk your melted butter, the brown sugar, and your honey until smooth. Add your egg yolk and the buttermilk; stir to combine.

Pour your dry mix over your wet and mix only until the flour has *just* disappeared. Don't overmix, or you'll end up with a cornbread brick.

Pour your batter in your loaf pan. Bake for 17-19 minutes. It's done when a toothpick comes out clean.

Let cool, then invert your loaf pan; your cornbread should pop right out. Slice and serve with a swirl of butter and some drizzled honey. Say hi to autumn.

You've Matcha Match Cookies
Alternative title: Matcha Matcha Man!

CaFae Latte has never been a place for soda (pop). Always coffee and tea. And our favorites are legion, but we always come back to the green. Off-topic, these green tea flavored cookies have a satisfying crunch but are chewy and tender inside. And they're a snap to make.

Ingredients:

- 2-1/2 teaspoons matcha (green tea) powder
- ½ teaspoon baking powder
- 1 teaspoon baking soda
- 2-3/4 cups flour
- 1 cup softened butter
- 1-1/2 cups granulated sugar
- 1 egg
- 1 teaspoon vanilla extract

Equipment:

- Cookie sheet
- Rubber spatula
- Small bowl
- Large bowl
- Wire rack

Directions:

Preheat your oven to 375 Fahrenheit. Grab your small bowl and mix your matcha, baking soda, baking powder, and flour. Set it aside.

In your large bowl, cream your butter and sugar until smoooooth. Add your egg and vanilla. Slowly add your dry ingredients.

Once everything is blended, scoop out your dough and roll it into a 1-inch ball. Put your balls on the sheet. Flatten slightly. If a certain fairy is trying to steal the dough, flatten a different set of balls.

As if you could.

Bake 8-9 minutes until golden. Let cool on your cookie sheet for 3-4 minutes before removing to your wire rack. This is the rare cookie that tastes better once it's all-the-way cool. Enjoy!

Chocolatey-orange/Orangey-chocolate Loaf

I dunno why orange + chocolate is only a thing at Christmas. It should always be a thing. Bake this for the 4th of July, dammit!

Ingredients:

- Zest of 2 oranges
- 1 teaspoon orange extract
- ¾ cup sugar
- ¼ cup brown sugar
- 1 teaspoon baking powder
- ½ teaspoon salt (use your vanilla salt!)
- 2 room temp eggs
- 1 cup Greek yogurt (or regular plain yogurt)
- ½ cup olive or vegetable oil
- 1 cup flour
- 1/3 cup cocoa powder (unsweetened)
- 1 of those weird chocolate oranges you can only find at Christmastime, chopped

Equipment:

- 9 x 5.5 inch loaf pan
- Large mixing bowl
- Whisk/rubber spatula
- Sifter

Directions:

Preheat your oven to 350 Fahrenheit. Grease or spray your loaf pan, then ignore it until you're damned good and ready.

Zest your oranges, then put the zest in your bowl with the sugar and intently rub 'em together like you're trying to figure out what the thread count is. Your sugar will get moist and orange and smell amazing.

Add your brown sugar, extract, and eggs to your zestified sugar. Whisk for about a minute until they're pale. Add your yogurt and oil; stir until combined.

Now sift your flour, baking powder, salt, and cocoa together and add to your wet ingredients. Fold gently until you can see just a few streaks of flour. Don't worry about small lumps and don't over-mix. Fold in your chocolate chunks.

Pour your batter into your loaf pan and bake for 45 minutes, or until a toothpick comes out clean as a whistle, because I guess whistles are historically clean? Cool on wire rack. Slice, enjoy, then go watch the fireworks.

About the authors

Author, TikToker, and overall feminist know-it-all, Christina Marie Alongi earned a bachelor's in history and social justice from Hamline University in 2017. Immediately after graduating, she worked as a community support staff (sort of a personal care assistant plus job coach) for adults with disabilities, including some of the autistic community, which helped inspire the main character for her debut sci-fi novel *Citadel*.

When she's not writing, reading, or content-creating, Alongi enjoys long walks, crocheting, and defending her furniture from her roommate's evil cat.

MaryJanice is the NYT and USA Today best-selling author of several novels and is published across multiple genres, including the *Undead* series and the upcoming *The Dim Reaper*. Her books have been published in over a dozen languages and have been on best-seller lists all over the world. She has published books, novellas, articles, short stories, recipes, reviews, and rants, and writes a bi-weekly column for USA Today.

A former model and medical test subject, she has been sentenced to live in St. Paul, MN, with her husband, children, and dogs.

Bibliographies

C.M. Alongi:

The *Blackwing* Series:

To Kill a Necromancer

Hetgarib's Curse

The Horned Guardian

Ghost Peak

The Slain Princess

Citadel (Minnesota Book Award Nominee)

The Witch Who Trades with Death (out March 2025)

MaryJanice Davidson

A Contemporary Asshat at the Court of Henry VIII

Derik's Bane

Wolf at the Door

The Undersea Folk (mermaids)

Sleeping With the Fishes

Swimming Without a Net

Fish Out of Water

The Déjà *Series (reincarnation)*

Déjà Who

Déjà New

The Alaskan Royals Trilogy

The Royal Treatment

The Royal Pain

The Royal Mess

The Gorgeous Books

Hello, Gorgeous!

Drop Dead, Gorgeous!

Doing It Right

Really Unusual Bad Boys

Under Cover

The Anthologies

I Have A Tapeworm (And Other Ways to Make Friends) (nonfiction)

Undead and Unmistakable: An Anthology of Nonsense

Wicked Women Whodunit

     (with Amy Garvey, Nancy J. Cohen)

Bad Boys With Expensive Toys

     (with Nancy Warren, Karen Kelley)

Merry Christmas, Baby

     (with Donna Kauffman, Nancy Warren, Erin McCarthy, Lucy Monroe, Susanna Carr)

Dying for You

Cravings

     (with Laurell K. Hamilton, Rebecca York, Eileen Wilks)

Bite

     (with Laurell K. Hamilton, Charlaine Harris, Angela Knight, Vickie Taylor)

Faeries Gone Wild

     (with Lois Greiman, Michele Hauf, Leandra Logan

No Rest for the Witches

     (with Lori Handeland, Cheyenne McCray, Christine Warren)

Kick Ass

(with Maggie Shayne, Angela Knight, Jacey Ford)

Men at Work

(with Janelle Denison, Nina Bangs)

Dead and Loving It

(with Janelle Denison, Nina Bangs)

Surf's up

(with Janelle Denison, Nina Bangs)

Mysteria

(with P. C. Cast, Gena Showalter, Susan Grant)

Mysteria Lane

(with P. C. Cast, Gena Showalter, Susan Grant)

Mysteria Nights

(with P. C. Cast, Gena Showalter, Susan Grant)

Over the Moon

(with Angela Knight, Virginia Kantra, Sunny)

Demon's Delight

(with Emma Holly, Vickie Taylor, Catherine Spangler)

Dead Over Heels

(with P. C. Cast, Gena Showalter, Susan Grant)

Perfect for the Beach

(with Lori Foster, Kayla Perrin, Janelle Denison, Erin McCarthy)

How To Be A Wicked Woman

(with Susanna Carr, Jamie Denton)

Charming The Snake

(with Camille Anthony, Melissa Schroeder)

The Shorts

Dead But Not Forgotten: Short Stories From The World of Sookie Stackhouse

My Angel, My Devil

Unwavering: A Betsy Short

LTF: A Satirical Romance

Keep You Brave And Strong: A Hurricane Harvey short

Sirena

Medical Miracle

Monster Love

Unreliable: A Betsy Short

Beggarman, Thief

Carrie

Titles by MaryJanice Davidson and Anthony Alongi

The Jennifer Scales series

Jennifer Scales and the Ancient Furnace

Jennifer Scales and the Messenger of Light

The Silver Moon Elm

Seraph of Sorrow

Rise of the Poison Moon

Evangelina

Made in United States
Troutdale, OR
11/22/2024